HANK WILLIAMS

For Ukulele

Cover photo by Photofest

ISBN 978-1-4584-9438-2

HAL•LEONARD®
CORPORATION

7777 W. BLUEMOUND RD. P.O. BOX 13819 MILWAUKEE, WI 53213

Visit Hal Leonard Online at
www.halleonard.com

CONTENTS

Baby, We're Really in Love

Words and Music by Hank Williams

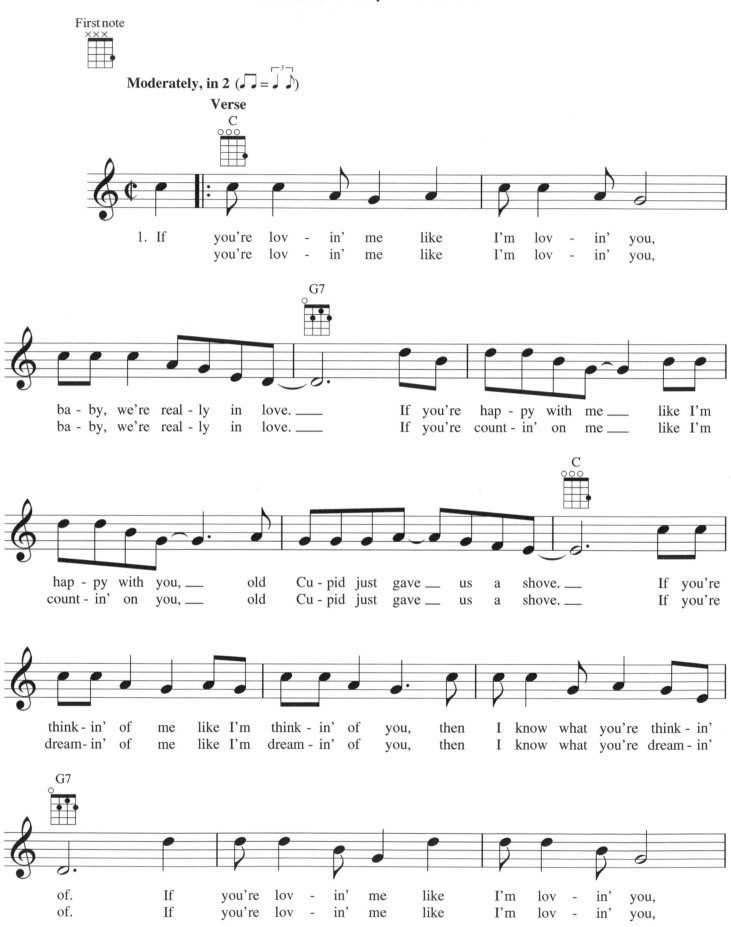

Cold, Cold Heart

Words and Music by Hank Williams

Verse
Moderately, in 2

1. I tried so hard, my dear, to show that you're my ev-'ry
(3.) nev - er know how much it hurts to see you sit and

dream. Yet you're a-fraid each thing I do is just some e - vil
cry. You know you need and want my love, yet you're a - fraid to

scheme. A mem - 'ry from your lone - some past keeps us so far a -
try. Why do you run and hide from life? To try it just ain't

part. Why can't I free your doubt - ful mind and melt your cold, cold
smart. Why can't I free your doubt - ful mind and melt your cold, cold

Half as Much

Words and Music by Curley Williams

First note

Verse

Moderately, in 2

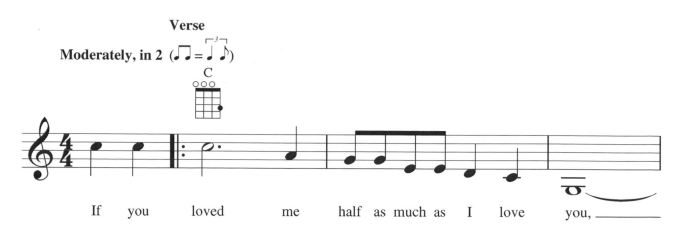

If you loved me half as much as I love you,

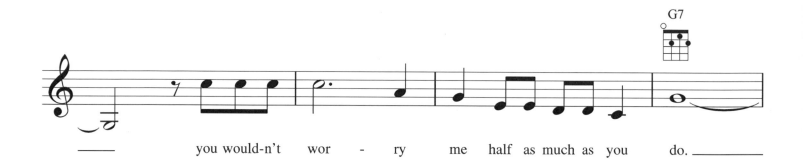

you would-n't wor - ry me half as much as you do.

You're nice to me when there's no one else a - round.

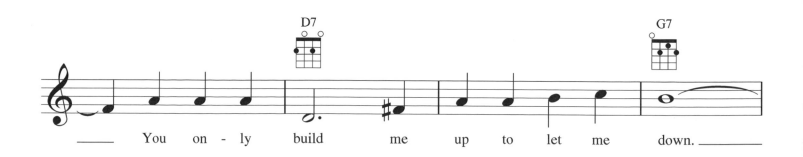

You on - ly build me up to let me down.

Chorus

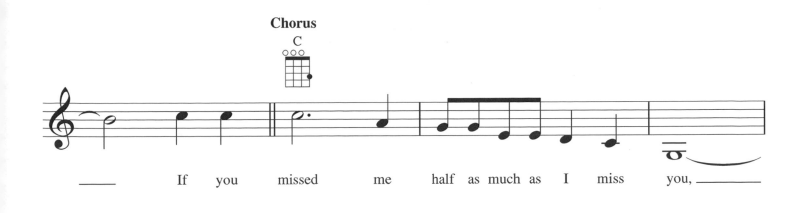

If you missed me half as much as I miss you, _____

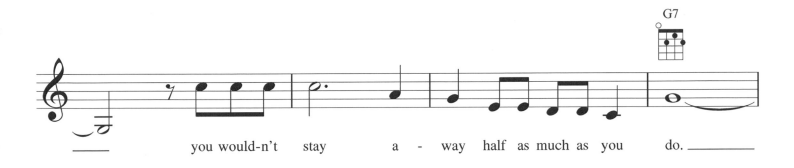

you would-n't stay a - way half as much as you do. _____

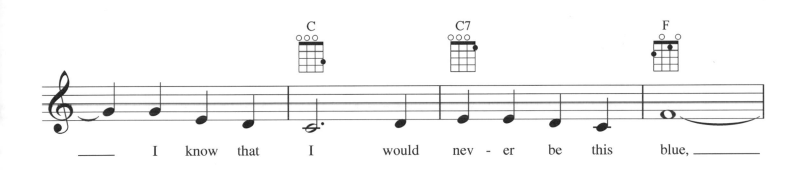

_____ I know that I would nev - er be this blue, _____

_____ if you on - ly loved me half as much as I love

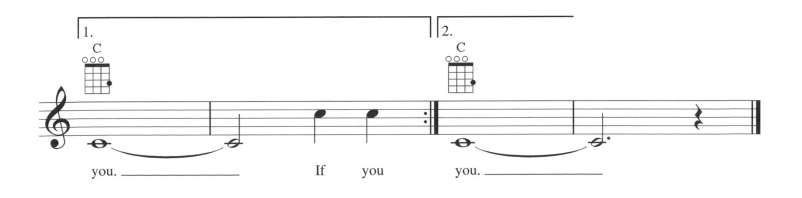

1.

you. _____ If you

2.

you. _____

Hey, Good Lookin'

Words and Music by Hank Williams

First note

Verse

Moderately fast

1. Hey, hey, good look-in', what - cha got
(2.) free and read - y, so we _____ can go

cook - in'? How's a - bout cook-in' some - thin' up ___ with
stead - y. How's a - bout sav - in' all your time ___ for

me? _____ Hey, sweet
me? _____ No more

ba - by, don't _____ you think may - be
look - in', I know _____ I've been took - en.

we could find us a brand - new rec - i - pe? _____
How's a - bout keep - in' stead - y com - pa - ny? _____

Bridge

I got a hot rod Ford and a two dol - lar bill, and
I'm gon - na throw my date - book _ o - ver the fence and

I know a spot right o - ver the hill. _ There's so - da pop and the
find me _ one for five or ten cents. _ I'll keep it 'til it's _

danc - in's free. _ So if you wan - na have fun, come a - long with me. _
cov - ered with age, _ 'cause I'm writ - in' your name down on ev - 'ry page. _

Chorus

Hey, good look - in', what - cha got

cook - in'? How's a - bout cook - in' some - thin' up _ with

1.
me? _ 2. I'm

2.
me? _

Honky Tonk Blues

Words and Music by Hank Williams

First note

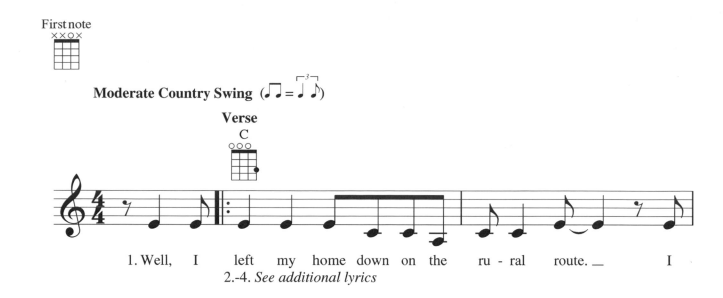

1. Well, I left my home down on the ru-ral route. __ I

2.-4. See additional lyrics

told my Paw I'm go-in' step-pin' out __ and get the

hon-ky-tonk blues, yeah, the hon-ky-tonk

blues. Well, Lord, __ I got 'em, __

_____ I got the hon - ky - tonk

blues.

2., 3. Well, I
4. I'm gon - na

Additional Lyrics

2. Well, I went to a dance and I wore out my shoes.
   Woke up this mornin' wishin' I could lose
   Them jumpin' honky-tonk blues, yeah, the honky-tonk blues.
   Oh, Lord, I got 'em, I got the honky-tonk blues.

3. Well, I've stopped into ev'ry place in town.
   The city life has really got me down.
   I got the honky-tonk blues, yeah, the honky-tonk blues.
   Well, Lord, I got 'em, I got the honky-tonk blues.

4. I'm gonna tuck my worries underneath my arm
   And scat right back to my Pappy's farm
   And leave these honky-tonk blues, yeah, the honky-tonk blues.
   Oh, Lord, I got 'em, I got the honky-tonk blues.

I Can't Help It
(If I'm Still in Love with You)

Words and Music by Hank Williams

I Saw the Light

Words and Music by Hank Williams

First note

Verse
Lively, in 2

1. I wan - dered so aim - less, life filled with

2., 3. *See additional lyrics*

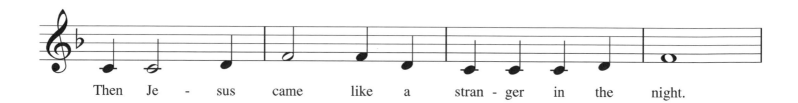

sin. I would - n't let my dear Sav - ior in.

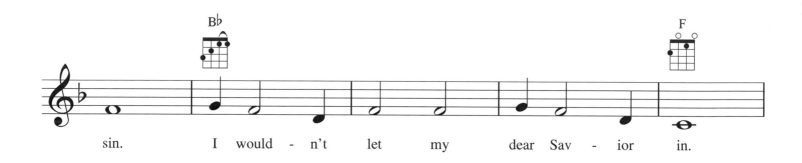

Then Je - sus came like a stran - ger in the night.

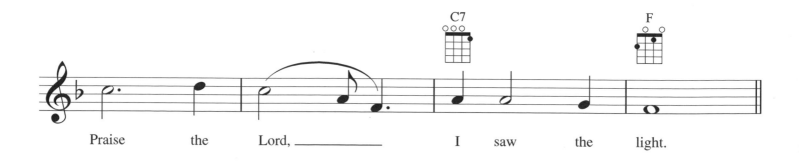

Praise the Lord, _____ I saw the light.

Chorus

I saw the light, _____ I saw the light, _____

no more _____ dark - ness, no more night. _____ Now I'm so

hap - py, no sor - row in sight. _____ Praise the Lord, _____

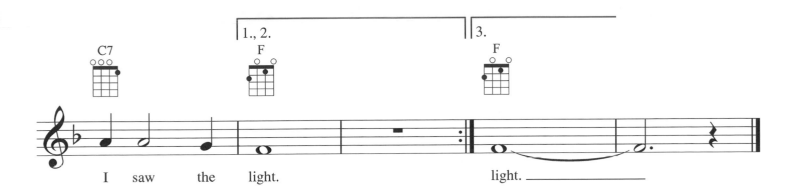

I saw the light. light. _____

Additional Lyrics

2. Just like a blind man I wandered along,
   Worries and fears I claimed for my own.
   Then like the blind man that God gave back his sight,
   Praise the Lord, I saw the light.

3. I was a fool to wander and stray,
   Straight is the gate and narrow is the way.
   Now I have traded the wrong for the right.
   Praise the Lord, I saw the light.

I'm So Lonesome I Could Cry

Words and Music by Hank Williams

1. Hear _____ that lone - some whip - poor -
(3.) ev - er see _____ a rob - in

will? He sounds _____ too blue _____ to fly. _____
weep when leaves _____ be - gan _____ to die?`_____

_____ The mid - night train is whin - ing
_____ That mid means he's lost the whin will to

low. I'm so lone - some I could _ cry. _____
live. I'm so lone - some I could _ cry. _____

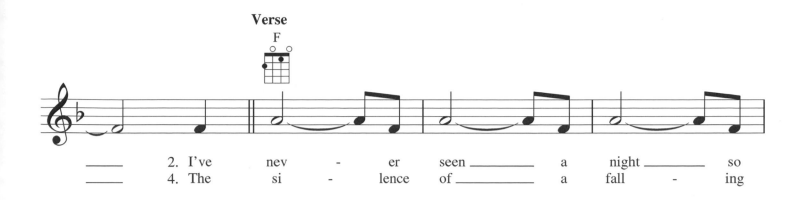

Verse

2. I've nev - er seen _____ a night _____ so
4. The si - lence of _____ a fall - ing

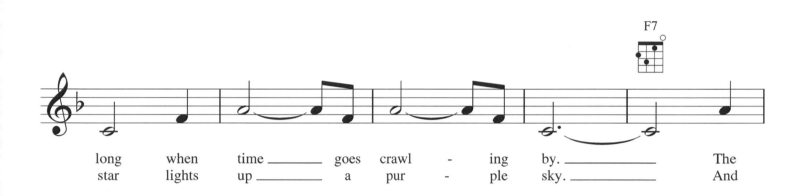

long when time _____ goes crawl - ing by. _____ The
star lights up _____ a pur - ple sky. _____ And

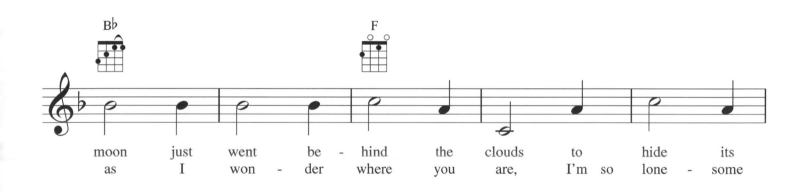

moon just went be - hind the clouds to hide its
as I won - der where you are, I'm so lone - some

face and ___ cry. _____ 3. Did you
I could ___ cry. _____

Jambalaya
(On the Bayou)

Words and Music by Hank Williams

Chorus

Jam - ba - la - ya, and a craw - fish pie, and fil - let

gum - bo. _____ 'Cause to - night I'm gon - na

see my ma cher a mi - o. _____ Pick gui - tar, ___

___ fill fruit jar, and be gay - o. _____

___ Son of a gun, we'll have big fun on the

1.

2.

bay - ou. _____ 2. Thi - bo - ___

Kaw-Liga

Words by Fred Rose
Music by Hank Williams

First note

Verse
Moderately fast, in 2

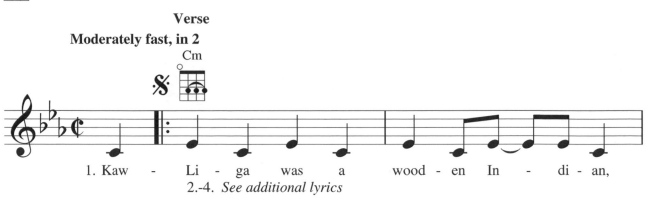

1. Kaw - Li - ga was a wood - en In - di - an,
2.-4. *See additional lyrics*

stand - ing by the door. ___ He fell in love with an

In - di - an maid - en o - ver in the an - tique store. Kaw -

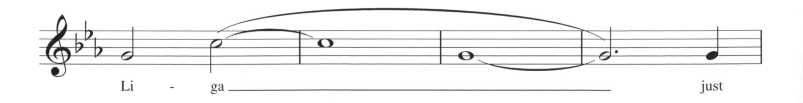

Li - ga ___ just

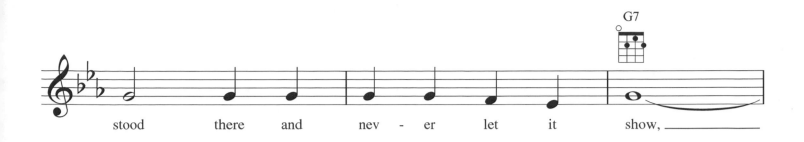

stood there and nev - er let it show, _____

_____ so she could nev - er an - swer "yes" or

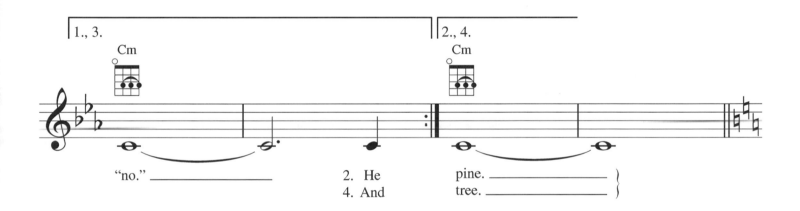

1., 3.
Cm
"no." _____

2., 4.
Cm
2. He pine. _____
4. And tree. _____

Chorus

C
Poor ol' Kaw - Li - ga, he nev - er got a kiss.

F
Poor ol' Kaw - Li - ga, he don't know what he missed.

Is it an - y won - der that his face is

To Coda ⊕

red? Kaw - Li - ga, that poor ol' wood - en

D.S. al Coda   ⊕ **Coda**

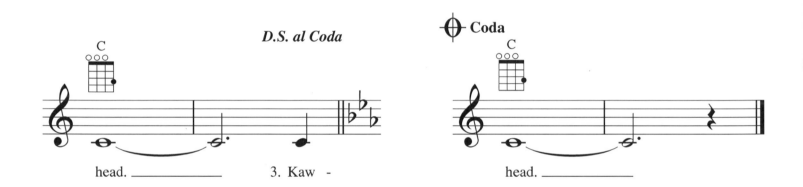

head. _____   3. Kaw -   head. _____

Additional Lyrics

2. He always wore his Sunday feathers and held a tomahawk.
   The maiden wore her beads and braids and hoped someday he'd talk.
   Kaw-Liga, too stubborn to ever show a sign
   Because his heart was made of knotty pine.

3. Kaw-Liga was a lonely Indian, never went nowhere.
   His heart was set on the Indian maiden with the coal-black hair.
   Kaw-Liga just stood there and never let it show,
   So she could never answer "yes" or "no."

4. And then one day a wealthy customer bought the Indian maid,
   And took her, oh, so far away, but ol' Kaw-Liga stayed.
   Kaw-Liga just stands there as lonely as can be,
   And wishes he was still an old pine tree.

I'll Never Get Out of This World Alive

Words by Fred Rose
Music by Hank Williams

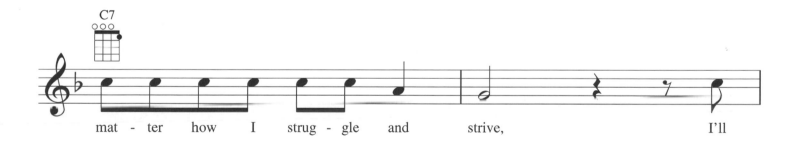

fish - in' pole is broke, the creek is full of sand. ___ My
it was rain - in' gold I would - n't stand a chance. _ I

wom - an run a - way with an - oth - er man. ___ }
would - n't have a pock - et in my patched - up pants. ___ } No

C7

mat - ter how I strug - gle and strive, I'll

F

nev - er get out ___ of this world ___ a - live. ___ { A
{ These

Bridge

B♭

dis - tant un - cle passed a - way ___ and
shab - by shoes I'm wear - in' all the time ___ are

F   F7

left me quite a batch. _____ And
full of holes and nails. _____ And,

Long Gone Lonesome Blues

Words and Music by Hank Williams

had   me   a   wom-an   who   could-n't   be   true;   she   made me for my mon-ey and she

told   me   on   Sun-day   she   was   check-in' me   out;   a - long a-bout   Mon-day she was

made   me   blue.   A   man needs a wom-an   that   he can lean on, ___   but my

no-where a - bout.   And   here   it   is Tues-day; ain't   had   no   news, ___   got them

Chorus

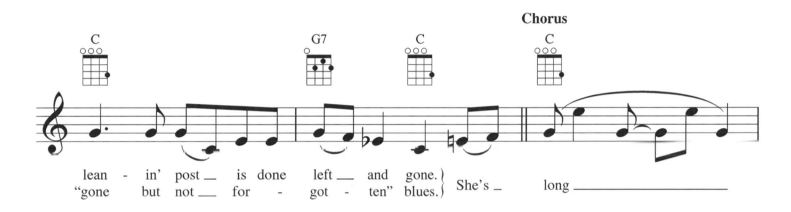

lean - in' post ___   is done   left ___ and   gone. }
"gone   but not ___ for - got - ten" blues. }   She's ___   long _____

gone _____   and   now _____   I'm   lone - some

1.   2.

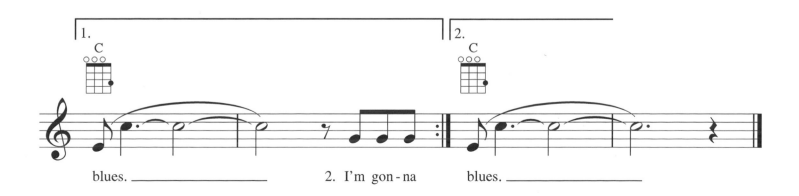

blues. _____   2. I'm gon-na   blues. _____

Moanin' the Blues

Words and Music by Hank Williams

First note

Verse

Moderately, in 2

1. When my ba - by moved out and the blues moved in, there was - n't
(3.) want a good gal to _____ stay a - round, you got to

noth - in' I could do but mo - sey a - round with my
treat her nice and kind. If you do _____ her wrong, she'll _____

head in my hands. Oh, what am I com - in' to? I just keep
leave this _____ town and you'll al - most lose your mind. Then you'll be

moan - in', _____ moan - in' the blues. _____ I
moan - in', _____ moan - in' the blues. _____ Oh,

Bridge

wrote a nice long let - ter _____ say - in', Ma - ma, please come
ba - by, ba - by, ba - by, _____ hon - ey ba - by, please come

My Bucket's Got a Hole in It

Words and Music by Clarence Williams

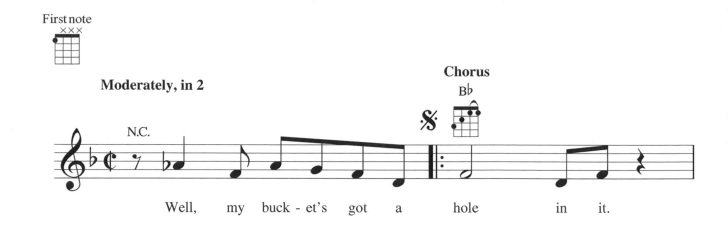

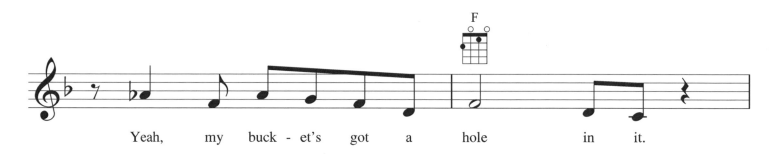

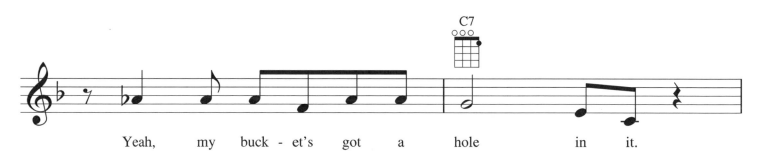

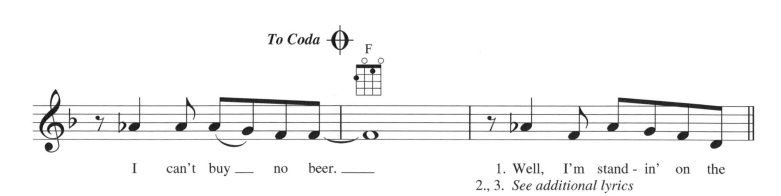

Additional Lyrics

2. Well, I went up on the mountain, I looked down in the sea.
   I seen the crabs and the fishes doin' the Bebop Bee.
   'Cause my bucket's got a... *(To Chorus)*

3. Well, there ain't no use of me workin' so hard,
   When I got a woman in the boss man's yard.
   'Cause my bucket's got a... *(To Chorus)*

Take These Chains from My Heart

Words and Music by Fred Rose and Hy Heath

First note

Verse
Moderately slow, in 2

1. Take these chains from my heart and set me free. _____
(3.) heart just a word of sym - pa - thy. _____

_____ You've grown cold and no long - er care for me. _____
Be as fair to my heart as you can be. _____

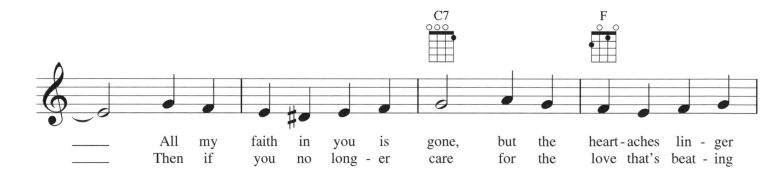

_____ All my faith in you is gone, but the heart - aches lin - ger
_____ Then if you no long - er care for the love that's beat - ing

on. Take these chains from my heart and set me free. _____
there, take these chains from my heart and set me free. _____

Verse

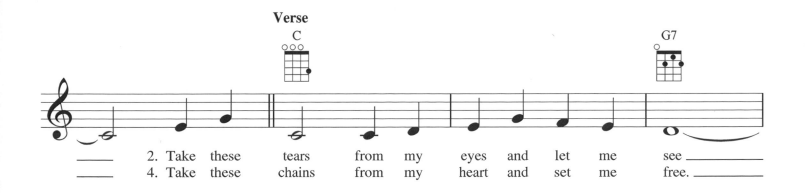

_____ 2. Take these tears from my eyes and let me see _____
_____ 4. Take these chains from my heart and set me free. _____

_____ just a spark of the love that used to be. _____
_____ You've grown cold and no long - er care for me. _____

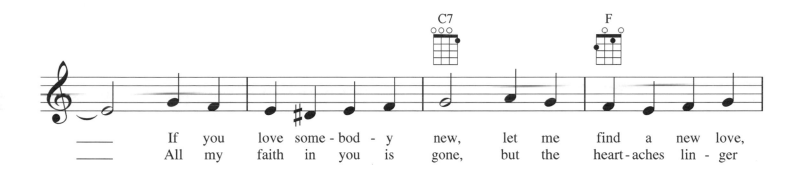

_____ If you love some - bod - y new, let me find a new love,
_____ All my faith in you is gone, but the heart - aches lin - ger

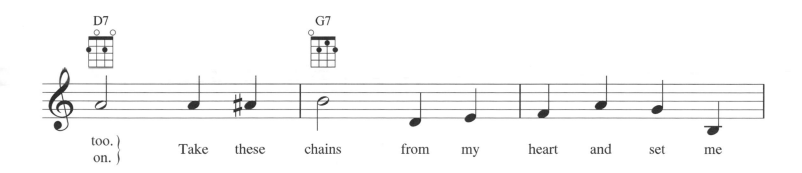

too. }
on. } Take these chains from my heart and set me

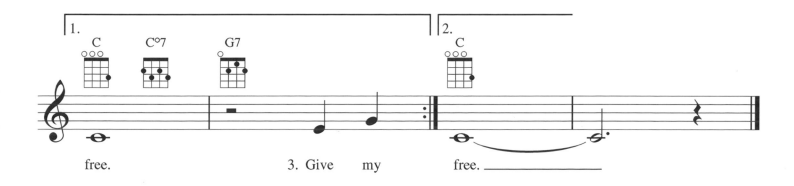

free.   3. Give my   free. _____

There's a Tear in My Beer

Words and Music by Hank Williams

First note

Verse

Moderately slow, in 2

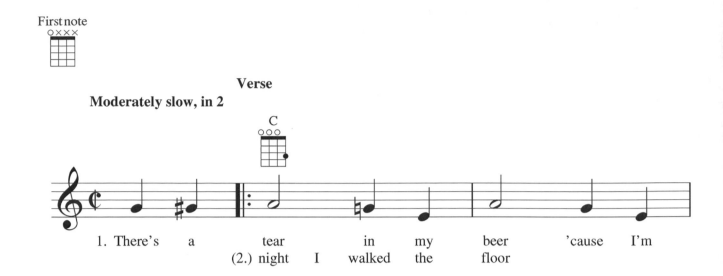

1. There's a tear in my beer 'cause I'm
(2.) night I walked the beer floor

cry - in' for you, dear. You are on my lone - ly
and the night be - fore. You are on my lone - ly

mind. _____ In - to these last nine beers I have
mind. _____ It seems my life is through and ___

shed a mil - lion tears. You are on my lone - ly
I'm so dog - gone blue. You are on my lone - ly

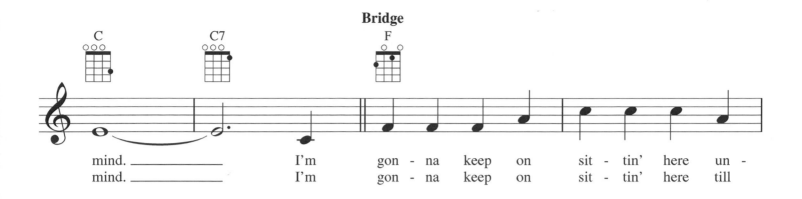

Bridge

mind. _____ I'm gon - na keep on sit - tin' here un -
mind. _____ I'm gon - na keep on sit - tin' here till

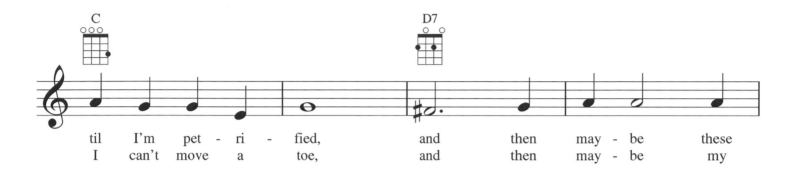

til I'm pet - ri - fied, and then may - be these
I can't move a toe, and then may - be my

Chorus

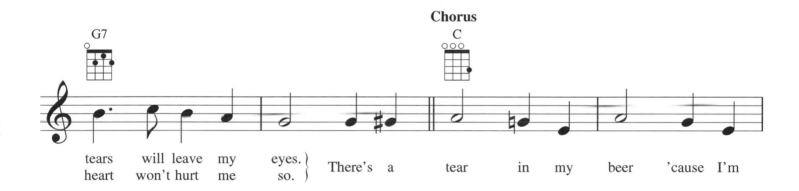

tears will leave my eyes. ⎫ There's a tear in my beer 'cause I'm
heart won't hurt me so. ⎭

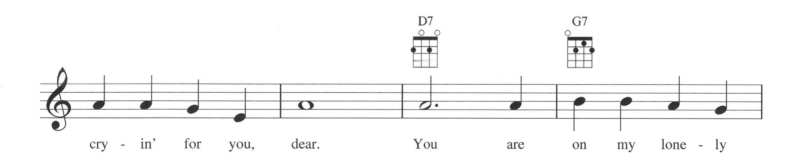

cry - in' for you, dear. You are on my lone - ly

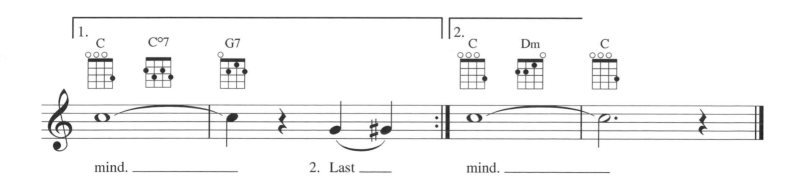

mind. _____ 2. Last _____ mind. _____

Why Don't You Love Me

Words and Music by Hank Williams

while. _____ We don't get near - er or fur - ther or

clos - er than a coun - try mile. _____

Chorus

{ Why don't you spark me like you used to do, _____ and
{ Why don't you say the things you used to say? _____

say sweet noth - ings like you used to coo? _____ I'm the
What makes you treat me like a piece of clay? _____ My

same old trou - ble that you've al - ways been thru, so
hair's still curl - y and my eyes are still blue.

1.
why don't you love me like you used to do? __ 2. Well,
Why don't you love me like you

2.
used to do? __

You Win Again

Wods and Music by Hank Williams

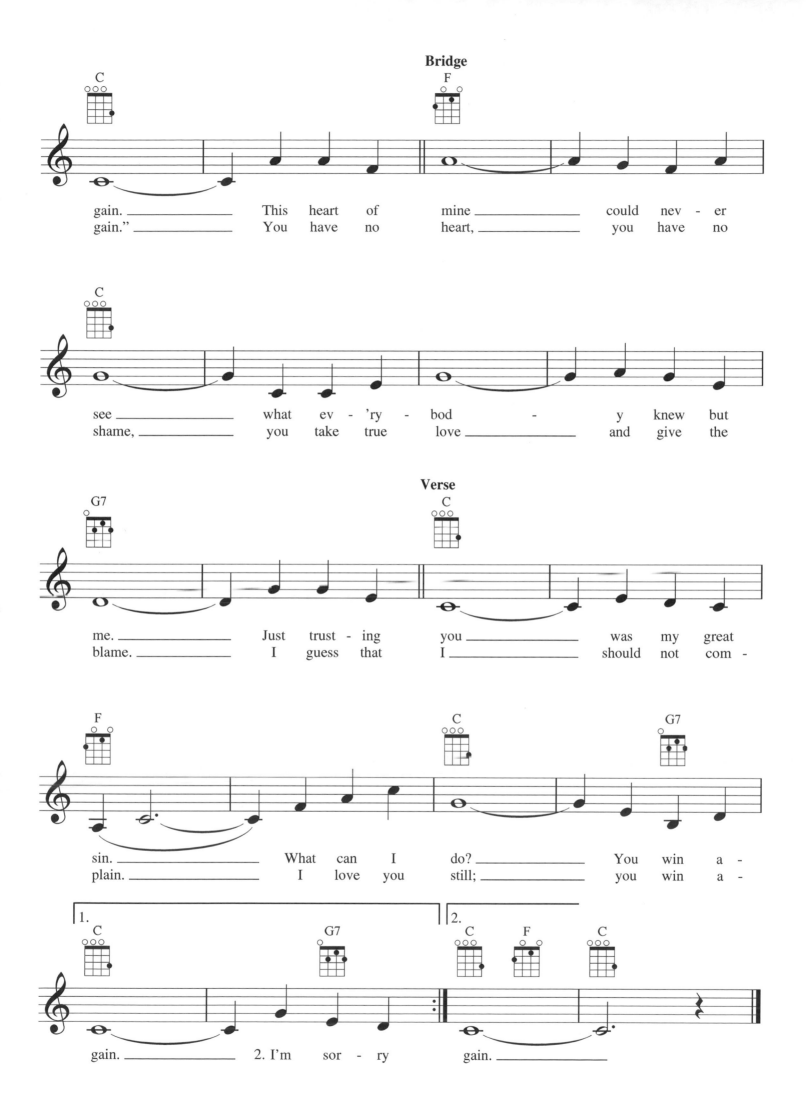

You're Gonna Change
(Or I'm Gonna Leave)

Words and Music by Hank Williams

Bridge

(1., 3.) You're gon - na change your way of liv - in',
(2.) The way to keep a wom - an hap - py and

change the things you do, stop do - in' all the things ___ that you
make her do what's right is love her ev - 'ry morn - in', bawl her

Chorus

ought - n't to. ___ } Your dad - dy's mad; ___ he's
out at night. ___ }

done got peeved. _____

You're gon - na change ___

___ or I'm a - gon - na leave. _____

leave. _____

Your Cheatin' Heart

Words and Music by Hank Williams

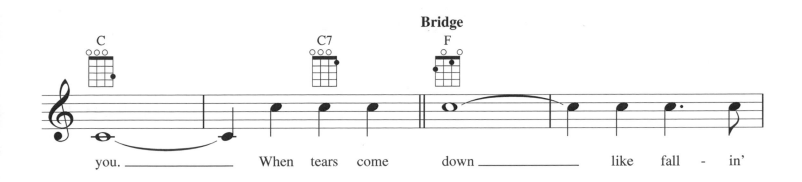

Bridge

you. _____ When tears come down _____ like fall - in'

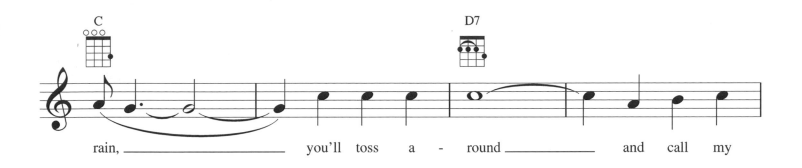

rain, _____ you'll toss a - round _____ and call my

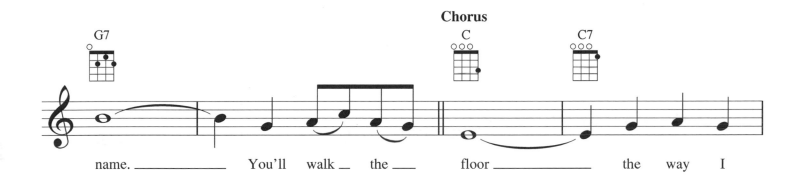

Chorus

name. _____ You'll walk _ the _ floor _____ the way I

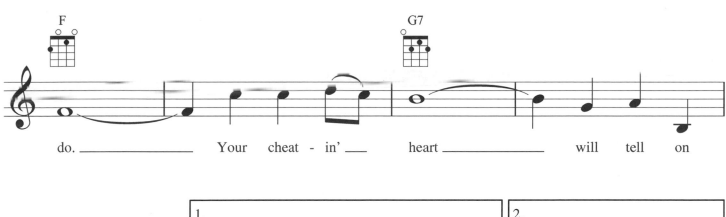

do. _____ Your cheat - in' _ heart _____ will tell on

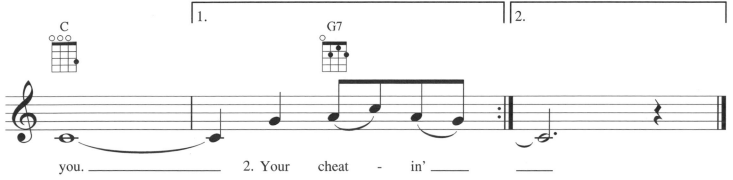

1. | 2.

you. _____ 2. Your cheat - in' _____ _____

HAL•LEONARD® UKULELE PLAY-ALONG

1. POP HITS
00701451 Book/CD Pack $15.99

3. HAWAIIAN FAVORITES
00701453 Book/Online Audio $14.99

4. CHILDREN'S SONGS
00701454 Book/Online Audio $14.99

5. CHRISTMAS SONGS
00701696 Book/CD Pack $12.99

6. LENNON & McCARTNEY
00701723 Book/Online Audio $12.99

7. DISNEY FAVORITES
00701724 Book/Online Audio $14.99

8. CHART HITS
00701745 Book/CD Pack $15.99

9. THE SOUND OF MUSIC
00701784 Book/CD Pack $14.99

10. MOTOWN
00701964 Book/CD Pack $12.99

11. CHRISTMAS STRUMMING
00702458 Book/Online Audio $12.99

12. BLUEGRASS FAVORITES
00702584 Book/CD Pack $12.99

13. UKULELE SONGS
00702599 Book/CD Pack $12.99

14. JOHNNY CASH
00702615 Book/Online Audio $15.99

15. COUNTRY CLASSICS
00702834 Book/CD Pack $12.99

16. STANDARDS
00702835 Book/CD Pack $12.99

17. POP STANDARDS
00702836 Book/CD Pack $12.99

18. IRISH SONGS
00703086 Book/Online Audio $12.99

19. BLUES STANDARDS
00703087 Book/CD Pack $12.99

20. FOLK POP ROCK
00703088 Book/CD Pack $12.99

21. HAWAIIAN CLASSICS
00703097 Book/CD Pack $12.99

22. ISLAND SONGS
00703098 Book/CD Pack $12.99

23. TAYLOR SWIFT
00221966 Book/Online Audio $16.99

24. WINTER WONDERLAND
00101871 Book/CD Pack $12.99

25. GREEN DAY
00110398 Book/CD Pack $14.99

26. BOB MARLEY
00110399 Book/Online Audio $14.99

27. TIN PAN ALLEY
00116358 Book/CD Pack $12.99

28. STEVIE WONDER
00116736 Book/CD Pack $14.99

29. OVER THE RAINBOW & OTHER FAVORITES
00117076 Book/Online Audio $15.99

30. ACOUSTIC SONGS
00122336 Book/CD Pack $14.99

31. JASON MRAZ
00124166 Book/CD Pack $14.99

32. TOP DOWNLOADS
00127507 Book/CD Pack $14.99

33. CLASSICAL THEMES
00127892 Book/Online Audio $14.99

34. CHRISTMAS HITS
00128602 Book/CD Pack $14.99

35. SONGS FOR BEGINNERS
00129009 Book/Online Audio $14.99

36. ELVIS PRESLEY HAWAII
00138199 Book/Online Audio $14.99

37. LATIN
00141191 Book/Online Audio $14.99

38. JAZZ
00141192 Book/Online Audio $14.99

39. GYPSY JAZZ
00146559 Book/Online Audio $15.99

40. TODAY'S HITS
00160845 Book/Online Audio $14.99

HAL•LEONARD®
www.halleonard.com

Prices, contents, and availability subject to change without notice.

The Best Collections for Ukulele

The Best Songs Ever

70 songs have now been arranged for ukulele. Includes: Always • Bohemian Rhapsody • Memory • My Favorite Things • Over the Rainbow • Piano Man • What a Wonderful World • Yesterday • You Raise Me Up • and more.

00282413 . . . . $17.99

Campfire Songs for Ukulele

30 favorites to sing as you roast marshmallows and strum your uke around the campfire. Includes: God Bless the U.S.A. • Hallelujah • The House of the Rising Sun • I Walk the Line • Puff the Magic Dragon • Wagon Wheel • You Are My Sunshine • and more.

00129170 . . . . $14.99

The Daily Ukulele

arr. Liz and Jim Beloff
Strum a different song everyday with easy arrangements of 365 of your favorite songs in one big songbook! Includes favorites by the Beatles, Beach Boys, and Bob Dylan, folk songs, pop songs, kids' songs, Christmas carols, and Broadway and Hollywood tunes, all with a spiral binding for ease of use.

00240356 Original Edition $39.99
00240681 Leap Year Edition $39.99
00119270 Portable Edition $37.50

Disney Hits for Ukulele

Play 23 of your favorite Disney songs on your ukulele. Includes: The Bare Necessities • Cruella De Vil • Do You Want to Build a Snowman? • Kiss the Girl • Lava • Let It Go • Once upon a Dream • A Whole New World • and more.

00151250 . . . . $16.99

Also available:

00291547 **Disney Fun Songs for Ukulele** . . . $16.99
00701708 **Disney Songs for Ukulele** $14.99
00334696 **First 50 Disney Songs on Ukulele** . $16.99

First 50 Songs You Should Play on Ukulele

An amazing collec-tion of 50 accessible, must-know favorites: Edelweiss • Hey, Soul Sister • I Walk the Line • I'm Yours • Imagine • Over the Rainbow • Peaceful Easy Feeling • The Rainbow Connection • Riptide • more.

00149250 . . . . $16.99

Also available:

00292082 **First 50 Melodies on Ukulele** . . . $15.99
00289029 **First 50 Songs on Solo Ukulele** . . $15.99
00347437 **First 50 Songs to Strum on Uke** . $16.99

40 Most Streamed Songs for Ukulele

40 top hits that sound great on uke! Includes: Despacito • Feel It Still • Girls like You • Happier • Havana • High Hopes • The Middle • Perfect • 7 Rings • Shallow • Shape of You • Something Just like This • Stay • Sucker • Sunflower • Sweet but Psycho • Thank U, Next • There's Nothing Holdin' Me Back • Without Me • and more!

00298113 . . . . $17.99

The 4 Chord Songbook

With just 4 chords, you can play 50 hot songs on your ukulele! Songs include: Brown Eyed Girl • Do Wah Diddy Diddy • Hey Ya! • Ho Hey • Jessie's Girl • Let It Be • One Love • Stand by Me • Toes • With or Without You • and many more.

00142050 . . . . $16.99

Also available:

00141143 **The 3-Chord Songbook** $16.99

Pop Songs for Kids

30 easy pop favorites for kids to play on uke, including: Brave • Can't Stop the Feeling! • Feel It Still • Fight Song • Happy • Havana • House of Gold • How Far I'll Go • Let It Go • Remember Me (Ernesto de la Cruz) • Rewrite the Stars • Roar • Shake It Off • Story of My Life • What Makes You Beautiful • and more.

00284415 . . . . $16.99

Simple Songs for Ukulele

50 favorites for standard G-C-E-A ukulele tuning, including: All Along the Watchtower • Can't Help Falling in Love • Don't Worry, Be Happy • Ho Hey • I'm Yours • King of the Road • Sweet Home Alabama • You Are My Sunshine • and more.

00156815 . . . . $14.99

Also available:

00276644 **More Simple Songs for Ukulele** . $14.99

Top Hits of 2020

18 uke-friendly tunes of 2020 are featured in this collection of melody, lyric and chord arrangements in standard G-C-E-A tuning. Includes: Adore You (Harry Styles) • Before You Go (Lewis Capaldi) • Cardigan (Taylor Swift) • Daisies (Katy Perry) • I Dare You (Kelly Clarkson) • Level of Concern (twenty one pilots) • No Time to Die (Billie Eilish) • Rain on Me (Lady Gaga feat. Ariana Grande) • Say So (Doja Cat) • and more.

00355553 . . . . $14.99

Also available:

00302274 **Top Hits of 2019** $14.99

Ukulele: The Most Requested Songs

Strum & Sing Series
Cherry Lane Music
Nearly 50 favorites all expertly arranged for ukulele! Includes: Bubbly • Build Me Up, Buttercup • Cecilia • Georgia on My Mind • Kokomo • L-O-V-E • Your Body Is a Wonderland • and more.

02501453 . . . . $14.99

The Ultimate Ukulele Fake Book

Uke enthusiasts will love this giant, spiral-bound collection of over 400 songs for uke! Includes: Crazy • Dancing Queen • Downtown • Fields of Gold • Happy • Hey Jude • 7 Years • Summertime • Thinking Out Loud • Thriller • Wagon Wheel • and more.

00175500 9" x 12" Edition $45.00
00319997 5.5" x 8.5" Edition $39.99

Order today from your favorite music retailer at
halleonard.com

Prices, contents and availability subject to change without notice

Disney characters and artwork TM & © 2021 Disney

UKULELE CHORD SONGBOOKS

This series features convenient 6" x 9" books with complete lyrics and chord symbols for dozens of great songs. Each song also includes chord grids at the top of every page and the first notes of the melody for easy reference.

ACOUSTIC ROCK

60 tunes: American Pie • Band on the Run • Catch the Wind • Daydream • Every Rose Has Its Thorn • Hallelujah • Iris • More Than Words • Patience • The Sound of Silence • Space Oddity • Sweet Talkin' Woman • Wake up Little Susie • Who'll Stop the Rain • and more.
00702482 . . . . $15.99

THE BEATLES

100 favorites: Across the Universe • Carry That Weight • Dear Prudence • Good Day Sunshine • Here Comes the Sun • If I Fell • Love Me Do • Michelle • Ob-La-Di, Ob-La-Da • Revolution • Something • Ticket to Ride • We Can Work It Out • and many more.
00703065 . . . . $19.99

BEST SONGS EVER

70 songs: All I Ask of You • Bewitched • Edelweiss • Just the Way You Are • Let It Be • Memory • Moon River • Over the Rainbow • Someone to Watch over Me • Unchained Melody • You Are the Sunshine of My Life • You Raise Me Up • and more.
00117050 . . . . $16.99

CHILDREN'S SONGS

80 classics: Alphabet Song • "C" Is for Cookie • Do-Re-Mi • I'm Popeye the Sailor Man • Mickey Mouse March • Oh! Susanna • Polly Wolly Doodle • Puff the Magic Dragon • The Rainbow Connection • Sing • Three Little Fishies (Itty Bitty Poo) • and many more.
00702473 . . . . $17.99

CHRISTMAS CAROLS

75 favorites: Away in a Manger • Coventry Carol • The First Noel • Good King Wenceslas • Hark! the Herald Angels Sing • I Saw Three Ships • Joy to the World • O Little Town of Bethlehem • Still, Still, Still • Up on the Housetop • What Child Is This? • and more.
00702474 . . . . $14.99

CHRISTMAS SONGS

55 Christmas classics: Do They Know It's Christmas? • Frosty the Snow Man • Happy Xmas (War Is Over) • Jingle-Bell Rock • Little Saint Nick • The Most Wonderful Time of the Year • White Christmas • and more.
00101776 . . . . $14.99

ISLAND SONGS

60 beach party tunes: Blue Hawaii • Day-O (The Banana Boat Song) • Don't Worry, Be Happy • Island Girl • Kokomo • Lovely Hula Girl • Mele Kalikimaka • Red, Red Wine • Surfer Girl • Tiny Bubbles • Ukulele Lady • and many more.
00702471 . . . . $16.99

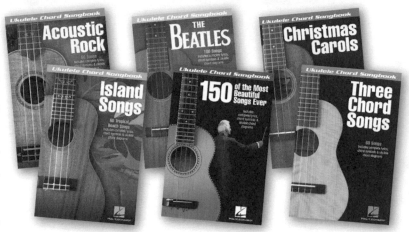

150 OF THE MOST BEAUTIFUL SONGS EVER

150 melodies: Always • Bewitched • Candle in the Wind • Endless Love • In the Still of the Night • Just the Way You Are • Memory • The Nearness of You • People • The Rainbow Connection • Smile • Unchained Melody • What a Wonderful World • Yesterday • and more.
00117051 . . . . $24.99

PETER, PAUL & MARY

Over 40 songs: And When I Die • Blowin' in the Wind • Goodnight, Irene • If I Had a Hammer (The Hammer Song) • Leaving on a Jet Plane • Puff the Magic Dragon • This Land Is Your Land • We Shall Overcome • Where Have All the Flowers Gone? • and more.
00121822 . . . . $14.99

THREE CHORD SONGS

60 songs: Bad Case of Loving You • Bang a Gong (Get It On) • Blue Suede Shoes • Cecilia • Get Back • Hound Dog • Kiss • Me and Bobby McGee • Not Fade Away • Rock This Town • Sweet Home Chicago • Twist and Shout • You Are My Sunshine • and more.
00702483 . . . . $15.99

TOP HITS

31 hits: The A Team • Born This Way • Forget You • Ho Hey • Jar of Hearts • Little Talks • Need You Now • Rolling in the Deep • Teenage Dream • Titanium • We Are Never Ever Getting Back Together • and more.
00115929 . . . . $14.99

Prices, contents, and availability subject to change without notice.

www.halleonard.com